D1709557

THE DROODLES TEN COMMANDMENTS STORYBOOK

RAY & SALLY CIONI
Color Renderings by Jerry Tiritilli

With comments to parents
and teachers by Edith Schaeffer

Table of Contents

For Dad:
honoring you was a privilege

1 You shall have no other gods before me.

2 You shall not make for yourself an idol in the form of anything in heaven above or on the earth beneath or in the waters below. You shall not bow down to them or worship them; for I, the Lord your God, am a jealous God, punishing the children for the sin of the fathers to the third and fourth generation of those who hate me, but showing love to thousands who love me and keep my commandments.

3 You shall not misuse the name of the Lord your God, for the Lord will not hold anyone guiltless who misuses his name.

4 Remember the Sabbath day by keeping it holy. Six days you shall labor and do all your work, but the seventh day is a Sabbath to the Lord your God. On it you shall not do any work, neither you, nor your son or daughter, nor your manservant or maidservant, nor your animals, nor the alien within your gates. For in six days the Lord made the heavens and the earth, the sea, and all that is in them, but rested on the seventh day. Therefore the Lord blessed the Sabbath day and made it holy.

5 Honor your father and your mother, so that you may live long in the land the Lord your God is giving you.

6 You shall not murder.

7 You shall not commit adultery.

8 You shall not steal.

9 You shall not give false testimony against your neighbor.

10 You shall not covet your neighbor's house. You shall not covet your neighbor's wife, or his manservant or maidservant, his ox or donkey, or anything that belongs to your neighbor.

Exodus 20: 3-17

Lenny Lumpkin Tunes Out

    If you're at all like me, you've watched television for as long as you can remember—maybe even longer. Lenny Lumpkin was like that. Every day from sunup to sundown, Lenny lived, loved, and breathed tv.

On the morning of our story, Lenny's alarm went off, as always, promptly at 6:30 A.M. With a yawn, Lenny dragged his worn-out blanket down the stairs, flipped the tv set on, then continued into the kitchen. He returned to his seat on the couch with a box of Frosted Koko-Nuts on his lap. By that time, the Arnold Aardvark cartoon show should have been on. But instead, the tv set was acting weird.

It made strange noises: *blip blip bleep bleep.* The picture looked like a painting he had seen at the modern art museum downtown.

Lenny fiddled with the tv knobs and slapped the side of the set. But he only managed to turn the picture from crossing guard orange to lightning bug green. He pressed his nose against the glass screen. "Mom, I don't feel so good," he moaned.

After one look at Lenny, his mother cried, "My poor baby!" Then she grabbed her overcoat and yanked him out the front door.

In the emergency room, Lenny deterio-
rated quickly. He babbled and blurted out blip-
ping and bleeping noises. His skin turned all
shades of orange and green. His eyes glowed like
twin fog lights.

Dr. Shurshot stepped in. "What seems to be the problem here?" he
asked, poking Lenny with several strange electronic instruments. After a
while, Lenny felt like poking back.

"Mrs. Lumpkin," the doctor said, removing his glasses, "I'm afraid he's
hooked."

"You mean—" she gulped.

"Yes." Dr. Shurshot sighed. "Videotosis. Lenny's mind is on the fritz."

Soon the room swarmed with masked and gloved assistants. They tested temperature, blood pressure, and pulse. Needles and tubes punctured Lenny in a dozen places. Nothing seemed to help.

"It's worse than we thought," said Dr. Shurshot. "We must operate immediately."

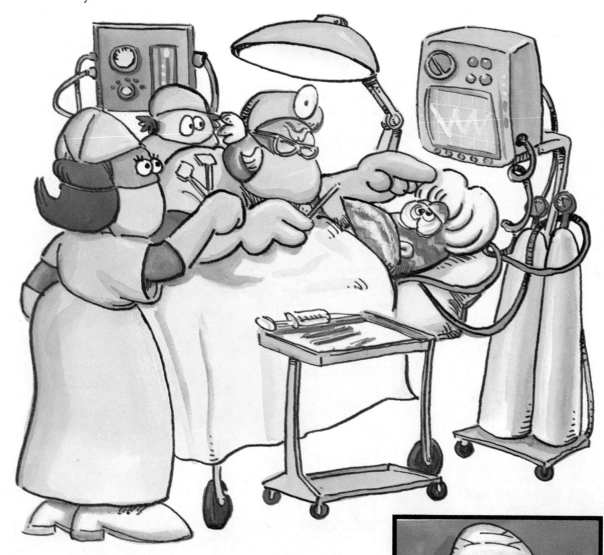

Under the skilled hands of Dr. Shurshot, the difficult operation went smoothly. Within hours Lenny was off the critical list, and a few days later he was sent home to recuperate. Soon he was back in Dr. Shurshot's office to have his bandages removed.

"Lenny's been such a good boy, Doctor Shurshot," exclaimed Mrs. Lumpkin. "He hasn't watched tv once since the accident."

"You know, we caught it just in time," the doctor replied, unfastening the bandage. "In extreme cases like this, a mind can tune out permanently!"

Dr. Shurshot smiled proudly as the last of the bandages was peeled off, revealing an antenna imbedded in Lenny's skull.

"Young man, you don't know how fortunate you are," the doctor explained. "From now on you need to explore the real world. Look at the wonders of nature, and above all make good friends. Put first things first!"

Lenny followed his doctor's advice. And, amazingly, the less he watched tv, the less he missed it. In fact, one morning he woke up to find his antenna crumpled on the floor. He was tuned in to better things.

And best of all, there were no commercials.

The First Commandment
You shall have no other gods before me.

Out of Focus

"Now, children," said Mom, "I know all about what happened last week. I realize Freddy was just using his slingshot to show how to kill a giant, and didn't mean to hit the window. And I know that when Bernard brought in the lawn sprinkler, he just meant to add realism to the Noah's ark skit. But please, let's try to pay attention in Sunday school today. OK, kids?"

"Oh, of course we will." "We always do." "Yes, what we learn here is very important."

"Well, tell me, kids," Mom asked, "how was Sunday school today?"

"Super!" "Great!" "Far out!" "Totally awesome!"

"Really?" Mom continued. "What was the lesson about?"

"Uh, well, that's a good question . . ."

"You tell her, Lucy. She's your mother."

"I think this guy ate a rotten apple. . . ."

"No, no, they put him in a lions' den!"

"Yeah, and then he went up a mountain with a headache to get some tablets. And then they made this golden moo-cow, and worshiped it."

"I see." Mother smiled skeptically. "Say, did you ever notice all the 'golden moo-cows' that block out what you ought to do at church?"

"Who, me?" "What is she talking about?" "I don't know, but I think we're in trouble. . . ."

The Second Commandment
You shall not make for yourself an idol . . . for I, the Lord your God, am a jealous God.

Marcia Branedrane's Name Game

Marcia Branedrane was the only child of Charles Foster Branedrane, the founder and president of the multinational corporation called Systematic Branedrane. (I'm sure you've heard of it.) One day, when Marcia's mother was sick in bed with the flu, Mr. Branedrane agreed to bring Marcia to work with him.

Soon their car pulled into Mr. Branedrane's reserved parking place beneath the Branedrane Building.

"Now, Marcia," he said, "I have meetings all morning, so just come to my office promptly at noon. And in the meantime, behave yourself. Remember, you're the president's daughter."

Marcia looked into his eyes. "Don't worry, Father. I won't let anyone forget it."

Mr. Branedrane got out of the car and hurried off toward the elevator. Marcia, who had three hours to get to the forty-second floor, decided to take the stairs. Inching open a heavy door, she found herself in a huge lobby. Hundreds of people crisscrossed the room, all in a hurry.

Marcia nudged her way into a crowd gathered at the snack counter. The clerk didn't even see her—until a little hand reached up and grabbed a pack of sugarless gum from the cardboard display.

"Hey, you!" snapped the woman behind the counter. "Where do you think you're going with that gum?"

Marcia was calm. "My daddy, Charles Foster Branedrane, said I could pick out anything I wanted," she answered.

"Your father is MR. BRANEDRANE?" the clerk gasped, handing the gum back. "Here, take it. It's on the house."

"Oh, thank you!" replied Marcia. "And I'll take a red licorice twist, too."

Candy in hand, she headed for the elevators. No sooner had the elevator doors slid shut than Marcia pushed every button from two to forty-two. By the sixteenth floor, she decided she needed a change of pace.

"Enough of this!" Marcia looked at the row of buttons on the elevator wall and pushed the red one that said EMERGENCY. *Clangg!!* The alarm rang out. Marcia scurried down the hall and found herself in a large room with eighty secretaries, all typing furiously.

She walked past several desks unnoticed, then spotted the lady who had been so nice to her at the company picnic.

20

"Hello, Charlotte," said Marcia smoothly. "I need you to type a letter for me. My daddy, Charles Foster Branedrane, said so."

"I'm sure he did," said Charlotte, doubting her every word.

"Would you like to ask him yourself?" Marcia challenged.

"No." Charlotte inserted a fresh white sheet into her typewriter.

Leaving Charlotte with a headache, Marcia took the letter and zipped down the hall, up two flights of stairs, and into a room marked Photocopy Center.

The room was empty except for one very large and expensive-looking copy machine. Standing on a chair, Marcia placed her letter on the glass plate and pressed the bright green COPY button. Bingo! *A perfect copy,* thought Marcia. *But you never know if one is enough.* She set the dial to 500, then skipped out the door.

On the thirtieth floor, Marcia tested the fire extinguishers. They worked.

On thirty-one, she pulled the fire alarm and then timed how long it rang before the fire department arrived to shut it off. Four minutes.

On thirty-two, she checked to see if the intercom was in good working order. It was, so she gave everyone in the building the afternoon off on behalf of her father, Charles Foster Branedrane.

She had worked up quite an appetite by noon. *Time for lunch,* she thought as she got back in the elevator and punched the top button.

In seconds the elevator door opened, revealing a woman seated behind a large desk. "Hello, Mrs. Stubbs," said Marcia sweetly.

22

"Miss Branedrane," said the secretary, "your father heard about your antics this morning. He says that you have some apologizing to do."

"No way!" Marcia roared. "Who does he think he is? He expects everybody to jump at the drop of his name! Mr. Branedrane wants *this*. Mr. Branedrane wants *that*. Blah! Blah! BLAH!"

"MARCIA!" She heard a familiar, but at the moment not very friendly, voice calling from the office behind Mrs. Stubbs. "Marcia Foster Branedrane. Step into my office right now. And close the door behind you."

Marcia gulped. Her name game was over— and she'd lost.

The Third Commandment
You shall not misuse the name of the Lord your God, for the Lord will not hold anyone guiltless who misuses his name.

Circuit Breakers

The NG-9000 had to give up its day off.
The owners remarked, "This will bring us more payoff."

But machines aren't made just to work
WORK
WORK.

Without time to recharge, this one went berserk!

The Fourth Commandment
Remember the Sabbath day by keeping it holy. Six days you shall labor and do all your work, but the seventh day is a Sabbath to the Lord your God.

Mother Knows Best

One day, not long ago, Bernard LaGordo found a frightened, long-eared creature shivering under his back porch. "Poor little fellow," said Bernard, gently reaching his hand under the first step. "You're cold and hungry, no doubt. And whew—do you need a bath!" The two went inside.

After a little food and a lot of suds, Bernard lifted his new friend to eye level. "You need a home," said Bernard, "and I've got one for you. You also need a name." Bernard thought of a few of his favorite things. "I'll call you Snackers."

Bernard provided a great home for Snackers. Every day after school, Snackers ran up the street to meet Bernard. And Bernard took Snackers with him everywhere: to the park, the store, even to a movie once. Bernard spent most of his spare time in the afternoons teaching Snackers all that he could. And Snackers quickly acquired Bernard's sweet tooth.

The day school let out for summer vacation was doubly special for Bernard. Not only did he never have to face Miss Oldenkrinkle again, but Snackers met him right at the school yard gate. He'd gotten there all by himself!

"Snackers!" laughed Bernard, feeding him a chocolate chewy-bite. "You're amazing!" Snackers licked Bernard's face, which Bernard liked most of all.

27

As the summer passed, Snackers grew bigger and bigger, smarter and smarter. Sometimes, while Bernard ate dinner, Snackers stayed out and went places on his own. He knew his way around so well that often he didn't come home until dark. Bernard always had a warm bath, a nice supper, and a sweet treat ready when Snackers came home. But he worried about his long-eared friend.

One night, late in the summer, Bernard sat on the back porch reading a comic book with a flashlight, waiting for Snackers. He stayed up far into the night. But still no Snackers.

Soon it was morning. Bernard's mother found him asleep on the back steps. "Bernard!" she cried. The screen door slammed behind her, and Bernard woke quickly. He glanced around the yard, hoping to see his little friend. But no Snackers. Bernard put his head in his hands.

"My poor baby," said Mrs. LaGordo. "Tell me what's wrong."

"I raised him and I fed him and I taught him," Bernard sniffled. "Now he's gone away, and he didn't even say good-bye. He didn't appreciate all I did for him."

"Sometimes that happens," said Mrs. LaGordo, sitting next to him.

Suddenly something important occurred to Bernard. "Mom," he said, "I really appreciate what *you* do for me."

Mrs. LaGordo hugged Bernard and kissed him on the nose. "You'll always be my little apple dumpling," she beamed.

"Aw, Mom," sighed Bernard, glad mostly that nobody was watching.

The Fifth Commandment

Honor your father and mother, so that you may live long in the land the Lord your God is giving you.

Jenny Jingles Strikes Out

After-school baseball is a favorite activity just about everywhere. And Troodleville is no exception. What better way can you think of to stretch fidgety, cramped muscles after a long day with Miss Oldenkrinkle?

Our friend Jenny Jingles wasn't much of a batter. But from her position in left field, she controlled the game. As the pitcher hurled the ball toward home plate, Jenny would let out the most powerful yell this side of King Kong. Her well-timed shriek usually left the batter too stunned to swing straight.

One day Jenny's team was on its way to another victory. That is, it was until Sugarlips Murphy stepped into the batter's box with a sneer on his face and a bag of gumdrops in his back pocket.

Ready Freddy Finstrom wound up for the pitch, winked at Jenny, and flung his famed fireball. Jenny let go with her loudest cry ever: *Eee-yaAAAAAH!*

But with scarcely a twitch, Sugarlips belted the ball into the bleachers.

"Thanks for the home run, Jenny," laughed Sugarlips. With a raspberry gumdrop stuffed in each ear, he hadn't heard her yell at all.

Sugarlips was paraded by his happy team down to Fudgelug's Sweet Shop. But Jenny's team felt like dragging her out to the city dump.

31

"I can't believe you let him do that, Jenny!"

"Yeah, Jingles, thanks a lot."

"Whose team are you on, anyway?"

"Next time, why don't you wear one of *their* uniforms?"

After several rounds of insults, Jenny let them have it right back. "ALL RIGHT ALREADY!" she screamed. "You can take your good-for-nothing team and go jump off Mount Rumblebog!"

You've probably heard the phrase, "If looks could kill. . . ." Well, that pretty much described Jenny's thoughts as she drifted off to sleep. That night she had a dream she would never forget. . . .

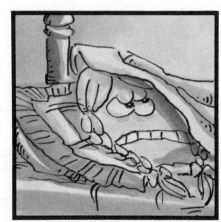

Jenny stared angrily out her bedroom window. She lifted the curtain. *There's that tubbo Bernard LaGordo riding his bicycle.* Remembering the game, her eyes burned with anger. Suddenly a blinding light arced across the front yard. When Jenny looked up again, Bernard was gone. His bike lay on the ground. *Where'd he go?* she wondered.

Moments later another figure strolled by. *Sugarlips Murphy!* she fumed. *That creep!* Then, as before, a flash of light streaked through the air toward Sugarlips. When Jenny's eyes recovered from the bright light, Sugarlips wasn't there.

First Bernard, now Sugarlips. Fear filled Jenny for a moment. *Just by looking at them?* Then she smiled. "Oh, boy!" she said, and dashed out the front door.

Every time she met someone she didn't like, *zappo*—they were gone forever. The lady that threw newspapers at Jenny whenever Jenny took the shortcut across her lawn. *Zappo.* The man with the mustache who never answered his doorbell on Halloween. *Zappo.*

And what about that no-good team of mine? thought Jenny. In her dream she raced over to the ball field, where everyone sat before school, trading baseball cards. "It's been nice knowing you," she scowled. Freddy, Lucy, Natalie, and all the rest disappeared instantly, like turning off a tv set.

This is a cinch! Jenny thought. *I've put all those undesirables in their places. Those goody-goody girls, Natalie and Lucy; that wisecracking whiz, Ready Freddy; that porkbelly, Bernard, and Sugarlips . . . Ooh!* She shivered. *He's the very worst!*

Then she looked back at the empty bleachers. *That Lucy sure loved animals, and Natalie is actually quite kind. And Freddy is always there when you need him, and then there's lovable old Bernard. . .*

Suddenly Jenny didn't feel so good. "Just who do I think I am?!" she cried.

And she woke herself up. It was morning, and the sun was streaming in on her face. She sat up with eyes opened wide. "What have I done?" She jumped to the window, and there was Bernard LaGordo riding his bike, just like before. He looked as alive as ever. "Bernard," she cried, "stay right there!"

Was it all a dream? Jenny wondered, darting through the living room. She flung open the front door and stared in disbelief.

"WE'RE SORRY!" boomed the voices of her teammates and other friends gathered huddled on Jenny's doorstep.

Sugarlips Murphy was at the very front. "Jenny," he said, "what good is life if people can't be friends?"

"It's no good at all," Jenny agreed, beaming as the gang lifted her up in the air and carried her off to school.

Lagging behind, Ready Freddy Finstrom nudged Bernard LaGordo. "And not only that," he said, "but I think we're all a lot safer with Jenny on our side."

The Sixth Commandment
You shall not murder.

Family Fitness

When moms and dads are true to each other,
Life is delightful for sister and brother.

But when fathers and mothers with others start flirting,
In no time at all the whole family is hurting.

The Seventh Commandment
You shall not commit adultery.

How Ready Freddy
Stole the Show

    "Science fairs. Yuk!" grumbled Ready Freddy Finstrom, kicking the front step of I. Q. Quigley's mansion. "Every year it's the same old drag. If it isn't reducing air pollution using moldy bread, it's generating electricity by burning potato peels. Now how is a busy person like me supposed to think up this stuff on his own?"

Ready Freddy was definitely not ready for tomorrow night's science fair. He hadn't even picked a topic. *I wish I could invent a robot to go instead of me,* he thought, ringing I. Q. Quigley's doorbell. *Oh well, I. Q. is always up to something. I'm sure he'll **inspire** me.*

"Frederick Finstrom," I. Q. said, smiling. "What brings you to my humble abode this evening? Returning the book you borrowed a year ago?"

"Not exactly," answered Freddy. "I just thought you might like some company tonight."

The two friends walked down the narrow staircase to I. Q.'s laboratory. Freddy stared at the jumbled collection of gizmos and contraptions before him, searching for an idea to take home.

"What's this, I. Q.?" he asked, picking up a little black box. "A new video game?"

"Careful, my boy. This is not for children!" I. Q. warned, grabbing the box back. "I call it TRAC-O-MATIC. It's a burglar alarm system that detects a thief and tracks him down by remote control."

"I see," Freddy said eagerly, anxious to hear more.

"No, you don't see," I. Q. explained. "You can't see it. Everything in a house protected by TRAC-O-MATIC is marked with an invisible electronic charge. Any stolen object gives off a signal that can be traced anywhere."

"You know, I. Q.," Freddy began, "you really ought to test your new invention. And the best place would be a spot likely to attract thieves."

"Quite right," I. Q. agreed.

"Well," Freddy continued, "my mother is on the prowl for a kitchen pirate who has been plundering desserts from our refrigerator."

"This would be highly irregular. . . ." I. Q. protested.

"So you're afraid it won't work, eh?" Freddy sneered.

"OF COURSE IT WORKS!" I. Q. shouted.

"Then it's all set," said Freddy, snatching the box. "I'll let you know what happens—next week."

As Freddy dashed through I. Q.'s front gate with his instant science project in hand, he bumped into a classmate. "Why, hello, Bernard," he said nervously. "What brings you to this part of town tonight?"

"I thought maybe I. Q. . . . uh . . . needed someone to talk to," stuttered Bernard. "Say, how is your science fair project coming?"

But Freddy was already halfway home.

Like Freddy, Bernard snooped around I. Q.'s lab, asking many questions. He showed a special interest in a miniature flying device. No sooner had I. Q. explained how it worked than Bernard remembered a scout meeting he was late for. The flying machine vanished with him.

I. Q. Quigley had never had so many guests in one evening. Each visitor seemed interested in a different experiment or invention. And many asked to borrow the one they liked most.

The science fair opened the next evening to a packed crowd. Bernard LaGordo stood by a poster that read Personal Flying Machines. Lucy Springbee's project was called Quirks of Quarks. Benny Bendswith sat proudly by Is There a Black Hole in Your Future?

The judges asked Ready Freddy Finstrom to begin the evening by demonstrating his original project, The Ultimate Anti-Theft Device. Freddy moved the switch on the black box to Track.

Suddenly, a deafening screech howled from the far corner of the room, and then from the other side, and then again from the front. Dozens of science fair projects sounded an ear-piercing alarm. Everyone froze helplessly, holding hands over ears.

Moments later—and none too soon—a small yellow hand reached around Freddy and, inserting a tiny key, turned off the black box. I. Q. Quigley glared angrily at all his visitors from the night before.

Nobody knew what to say until, with a grin, Freddy broke the silence. "Well, I. Q., at least we know one thing."

"What's that?" I. Q. snapped.

"It works!"

The Eighth Commandment
You shall not steal.

Gloria Tattletooth Talks Up a Storm

"I do so love birthday parties!" said Gloria Tattletooth to Natalie Creampuff. Together they were creating a triple luscious lemon layer cake in Natalie's kitchen.

"Yes, especially a party for such a terrific fellow as Ready Freddy Finstrom," sighed Natalie. "I want to make this my very best cake ever. Remember how Freddy helped me sell Goody Girl Club cookies last spring? What a guy."

"Sure. But didn't he eat twice as many as you sold?" Gloria interrupted, sifting some flour into a mixing bowl.

"Well, that's a minor detail," Natalie said, "for someone as generous as Freddy."

"Yeah." Gloria Tattletooth rolled her eyes. "He's sure overwhelmed Jenny Jingles with his generosity lately."

"Don't be ridiculous," Natalie snapped, cracking an egg on the side of the bowl. "I don't even want to hear about Jenny and Freddy."

"Fine with me," Gloria agreed. "Besides, Freddy's too smart to *really* fall for a big mouth like her."

"How do you know Freddy does so much with Jenny?" Natalie cracked another egg, this time dropping the shell into the bowl. "Why, he volunteered to help Old Man Henkel with his yard work, and that takes up most of his spare time."

"Volunteered? My foot!" said Gloria. "He's probably draining the old geezer's checkbook."

"How much money do you think he spends on Jenny?" Natalie asked, tossing several more eggs and a dozen whole lemons into the batter.

"Well, with all the money he wastes on junk food and comic books," Gloria began, "he probably doesn't have much left for Jenny, but—"

"Boy, what a creep!" fumed Natalie, shoving the whole lumpy cake into the oven.

It baked in no time. Gloria added oodles of frosting, while Natalie sat staring into space, thinking angry thoughts. Just then, the doorbell rang.

"It's that lousy, no-good, self-serving two-timer, FREDDY!" sputtered Natalie, carrying the cake to the front door.

Freddy poked his head through the doorway. "For me?" he grinned.

"HAPPY ROTTEN BIRTHDAY!" shouted Natalie, dumping the cake onto Freddy's head.

"My favorite: upside-down cake," said Freddy, peering through dripping layers of eggshells, lemons, and buttercream frosting. "What did I do to deserve this?"

"Don't get me started!" said Natalie, slamming the door in his face.

"What did I do?" Freddy repeated.

Gloria shrugged. "I don't know what came over her. She has *such* a temper."

The Ninth Commandment
You shall not give false testimony against your neighbor.

51

A Million Toys Too Many

By the time that Christmas vacation ends, most of the young folks in Troodleville feel real grumpy. The holiday cheer has been tossed out along with the torn wrappings of disappointing gifts.

"You know that Gabby Gertie doll they show all the time on tv?" scowled Lucy Springbee just before class. "Well, the one I got only says twelve things. Big deal."

"I gave my baby sister this really great remote control race car," explained Ready Freddy Finstrom. "And you know, it really wasn't all that great."

"Hey, there's that new kid who moved in at Christmas," said Sugarlips Murphy, pointing his peppermint stick toward the only quiet person in the classroom. "Let's ask what he got."

"Allow me," said Freddy, leaning over toward the visitor. "HEY, NEW KID!" yelled Freddy. "YOU GOT TOYS?"

"Yes," the boy answered politely. "And I also have a name: Gilman Chatsworth."

"Everybody listen up: Gilman here's got toys," Freddy proclaimed. "What kinds of toys do you have, Gilman?"

Again, Gilman replied courteously. "Actually, I have a room with a million toys."

"Ha! I'll bet you do," Freddy scoffed. "Did your father rob a bank?"

"No," smiled Gilman. "He owns one. In fact, he owns several. If you like, you may all come to my house after school today to play."

The class was stunned.

Invitations like that happen once in a lifetime, at most. Before they knew it, school ended, and they stood inside the Chatsworth mansion facing the massive doors to Gilman's playroom.

"Welcome, friends," smiled Gilman, pushing a green button marked Open. "All that is mine is yours to enjoy."

And enjoy they did.

From then on, every day after school the whole gang headed for Gilman's place. Their own toys, even their favorites, soon lay at home forgotten. Each day they played until their mothers called them home. And each night they drifted off to sleep wishing for more and better toys at Gilman's.

"Say, Sugarlips," called Ready Freddy one day, whizzing around Gilman's playroom on a Roller-Go-Cart. "Have you ever noticed that Gilman never comes in here with us?"

"Come on," Sugarlips howled, rounding the next curve. "This place is so big, how can you be sure?"

"I'm sure," Freddy insisted. "Gilman always leaves us off at the door. I think he has another playroom somewhere just for himself. And it's probably twice as big as this one."

"A SUPER ROOM?" The very thought overwhelmed Sugarlips.

From then on, Freddy and Sugarlips had a tough time enjoying Gilman's playroom. No matter what toy they played with, the thought that there was an even more spectacular collection elsewhere left their mouths watering.

One afternoon, as the rest of the gang entered the playroom, Freddy and Sugarlips stayed by the door.

"Look, Gilman, old chum," said Freddy, putting his arm around Gilman's shoulder, "we know you've got something else going on around here somewhere. You never play in here yourself."

"Yeah," Sugarlips agreed. "You haven't shown the slightest interest in anything in that big room. We think you're holding back on us." The two edged close to Gilman. "Show us your secret room!" they demanded.

Nervously, Gilman led them through a long passageway lined with portraits of old men, then down a long stairway crowded with portraits of old ladies. Finally he stopped at an old iron door, pulled a large brass key from his pocket, and turned it in the rusty lock. The door creaked, and blinding sunlight shone into the dark stairwell.

"I don't believe my eyes!" Freddy gasped.

"It can't be true!" gulped Sugarlips, choking on a fudgedrop.

In front of them lay a tiny, grass-covered courtyard with an ordinary oak tree in the center. A tire swing dangled from one branch, and a rickety ladder led to a tree house.

"You mean this is where you play?" Freddy exclaimed. "This little weed patch?"

"Yes. Here I can be anyone: a pirate, a soldier, a knight in King Arthur's court," Gilman explained. "I can explore jungles, sail the oceans, or go to the moon. I've discovered that my imagination is better than anything money can buy. And it doesn't cost a dime."

Gilman ran over to his tree and, with one foot on the bottom of the ladder, called back, "Wanna play?"

Sugarlips and Freddy looked at each other, then giggled. "Sure, Gilman, why not?"

The Tenth Commandment
You shall not covet your neighbor's house. You shall not covet your neighbor's wife, or his manservant or maid-servant, his ox or donkey, or anything that belongs to your neighbor.

Tips for Parents and Teachers

"Your hands made me and formed me; give me understanding to learn your commands" (Psalm 119: 73).

In our times, when children are being taught that there is no one "out there" at home in the universe, that no Creator made them because the universe came about by chance, it naturally follows that there are no eternal commandments. In a child's logical mind, if no Creator exists, there is no one to have given commands. The Ten Commandments become quaint, old-fashioned ideas that some human beings made up—and that are now quite out-of-date. So why bother with them?

If there is no God whose commands never change, then everyone can do what is right in his or her own eyes. That, of course, is what people are doing today. From newspapers and schoolmates, children discover that it is OK to do one's own thing, that right and wrong are constantly changing. In many schools, they are taught that there is a great diversity of "right" ways.

"Oh," you say, "but our family (or class) is different, because I do believe God exists. The children in my care have an alternative teaching." Do they? If you were swimming upstream in a strong current, with your children behind you like ducklings following mama and papa duck, wouldn't you look around and warn them of bad whirlpools or submerged rocks ahead that might hurt them? When the current is dangerous, children need help constantly—and the adults caring for them also need to be alert to dangers to themselves.

Such a current swirls around all of us today through television, newspapers, and magazines, and from the lips of those we meet. We're apt to be caught up in thinking that, after all, what the majority feels must be right, everyone's doing it, and so on. Even believers may be pulled by the tide. Many who think of themselves as faithful children of God nevertheless feel that the Ten Commandments belong to history, and are not to be central in today's life-style.

This is nothing new. If you'll remember, the first people to turn their backs on God and his commandments were the people of God, the Israelites. At the foot of Mount Sinai, they were dancing around the golden calf, a false god they had made, and were worshiping in an orgy of pleasures, rather than eagerly waiting to discover what the eternal, infinite, unchanging God was going to tell them.

What is pleasing to God is impressing the commandments on our minds, translating them into action. Since human beings are created by God, in the image of God, it is God himself who understands human beings. To live on the basis of his commandments is not to be deprived of fun, but to have true fulfillment opened to us. Only tragedy results from living on the basis of something else.

You can prevent future tragedies of choice for your children and yourself by becoming familiar with all the wonders of the Ten Commandments. Am I speaking about simply reciting them by memory in a singsong voice? No! They merit much closer study, as I have learned myself. Inspired by Ray Cioni's interest in making the

Ten Commandments vital for today, and urged on by my son Franky, I recently studied them myself and wrote *Lifelines* (a book adults should read while their children are reading this Droodles book).

As I searched the Bible and wrote that book, I was humbled and astonished at all the choices and actions in daily living that involve the Ten Commandments. How easy it is not to recognize that we are breaking them! So thoroughly do they form a framework for living that it is necessary to read and reread them.

Ray and Sally Cioni have created an imaginary people, the Droodles, who first captured the interest of many children in *The Droodles Storybook of Proverbs.* They have been looking for the next Droodles book, and here it is! Now Ray and Sally have used the Droodles to "throw ice water" and awaken children to seeing that God's commandments affect their daily choices in playing and studying, in big and little things. The Droodles are plunged into situations you can use to spark thoughts and questions about God's commandments in other life situations today.

When your child reads or hears the story "Lenny Lumpkin Tunes Out," for example, you will of course be asked to read it again and again! But you can also talk about what other things (besides Lenny's television) can usurp the special place God is meant to have in our lives. In "Out of Focus," you can talk about objects, thoughts, and activities that replace God as our focus in a worship situation. After reading about Marcia Branedrane, you can discuss that God's name should be used to accomplish what God wants—not as a cover-up for our own desires.

The important task is to continue with discussion after reading a story, and to be ready to take what is between the covers of the book out into your own family life or classroom. Add to what is in the book with further study and imagination. Let the children write or draw pictures to illustrate a commandment applied to their own lives. For example, they could draw a picture of a situation in which they are tempted to steal—either to steal an object, or to steal someone else's idea and claim it for one's own, as Ready Freddy does. After reading "Jenny Jingles Strikes Out," children could write a list of those with whom they get so angry that they commit murder in their hearts. Then they could try to learn, as Jenny learned, the value of each and every person in God's eyes.

I also suggest that you add to your family or classroom study of the commandments by reading from Psalm 119, a rich source. Ask God honestly that you be able to desire what the psalmist desired in Psalm 119:172: "May my tongue sing of your word, for all your commands are righteous." We can ask this with sincerity, and with excitement, because God has given us the framework for a fulfilling life.

Edith Schaeffer
L'Abri Fellowship
Huemoz, Switzerland